I0820091

Bright
Light
Hardie Grant Children's Publishing
Inda Ahmad Zahri
Syd Fini
OUR VOICES,
TOGETHER

We heard your distant call today.
Your voice was small but brave.
It pierced the dust and rubble
of the homes you tried to save.

Your laughter that was tossed aside,
the cheer snatched from your hands,

lay on the ground like broken toys
when war came to your lands.

But still, your strong and fearless voice
gives courage to our own.

This fight of yours is our fight, too,
and you won't be alone.

We'll shout away the bombs and drones –
the menace in your skies.

Imagine armies shrinking from
the might of all our cries.

We'll thunder as the tanks roll in.
Your homes should not be crushed!

Your childhood songs
and happy, playful chants
should not be hushed.

We'll sing in open spaces
and in every market square.

We'll wave our banners, slogans,
flags and hands up in the air.

We'll march our voices to the beat,
down every busy street.

The ground will shake and stir beneath so many little feet.

We'll splash our words on big, bold signs.
We'll chant them as we walk.

We'll paint the walls with signs of peace,
so even stones can talk.

We'll echo in the chambers
where important votes are cast.
WE ARE ALL ONE
WE STAND WITH YOU
PEACE ON EARTH

حب
PEACE
We'll ask them
for a safer world,
tell them we
need it fast.

And when we need a rest,
as even strongest voices might,

we'll hold you softly in our hearts,
by silent candlelight.

We hear you.
We see you.
We're with you.
Don't give up!
So long as we still have a voice,
we won't stop speaking up.

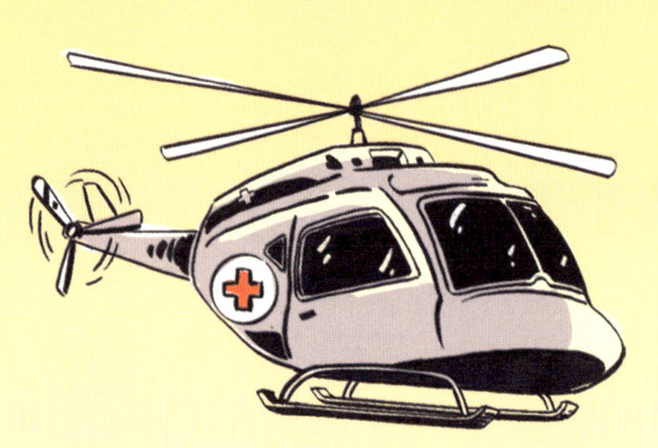

There will be those who hear our cries
and take our words to heart.

They'll share them in their actions,
in their speeches, in their art.

VOICES FOR TRUTH
NO WAR
YOU ARE NOT ALONE
PEOPLE POWER

Together, then, our words will grow
into a massive wave,
to wash the fighting from your lives,
so precious and so brave.

A silence can be broken
by the might of one small word.

Our voices are our power ...

HUMAN RIGHTS ARE FOR EVERYONE
WE ARE ALL ONE
NO WAR
NO MORE OMBS
RAISE YOUR VOICE
FREEDOM! FREEDOM! FREEDOM!
WE STAND WITH YOU
PEACE ON EARTH

... and together we'll be heard.

To all children, the souls of our souls. ~ I.A.Z.

To my sister, Minoo. ~ S.F.

Hardie Grant acknowledges the Traditional Owners of the Country on which we work, the Wurundjeri People of the Kulin Nation and the Gadigal People of the Eora Nation, and recognises their continuing connection to the land, waters and culture. We pay our respects to their Elders past and present.

Bright Light,
an imprint of Hardie Grant Children's Publishing
Wurundjeri Country
Level 11, 36 Wellington Street
Collingwood Victoria 3066
Melbourne | Sydney | San Francisco

hardiegrant.com/childrens

ISBN: 9781761211249
First published 2026

A catalogue record for this book is available from the National Library of Australia

Publishers Alyson O'Brien and Pooja Desai **Design** Pooja Desai
Editorial Joanna Wong and Claire Davis with Luna Soo **Production** Sally Davis

Printed and bound in HeShan China, October 2025, by LEO Paper Products LTD.

The paper this book is printed on is from FSC® certified forests and other controlled sources. FSC® promotes environmentally responsible, socially beneficial and economically viable management of the world's forests.

2 4 5 3 1

Dear young reader,

I wrote this story in 2021, when Gaza was attacked again. Heartbroken, I watched news of families with young children harmed by acts of war. I hugged my own children tight, grateful to live in peace and safety, but angry that children elsewhere did not have their rights protected.

As you learn of wars around the world, you'll rightly have questions for us grown-ups. We might not have all the answers, but I hope you know that every child, including you, deserves to be loved. That's a truth we'll fight to uphold, even if all we have are our voices.

Your own young voice is precious and powerful. By speaking up, we can stop those who want us to stay silent so that bad things can keep happening. We can also echo the voices of children forced into war, and let them know they're loved and not ignored or forgotten.

Whether you are speaking from the chaos of war or in peaceful solidarity, your voice matters. This is for you.

Inda

Hi,

I'm a graphic novel artist and animation director, and for as long as I can remember I've been illustrating scenes of war. I grew up in Iran during the eight-year war in the 1980s, and the impact of that time has stayed with me.

When I first read Inda Ahmad Zahri's story *Our Voices, Together*, something shifted in me. It wasn't just about the pain or loss anymore; it was about hope. Her words opened up a new way of thinking for me: even in the face of conflict, we can imagine something better.

As I illustrated Inda's story, I thought deeply about children. What they lose in war, but also what they still carry: imagination, strength and the ability to rebuild. I wanted to show that yes, war is devastating, but there's always something we can do.

Drawing this book became a kind of quest. Not just to depict war, but to offer a glimpse of resilience. It reminded me that telling stories like this can be a way to heal, remember and move forward. Together.

Syd